Carl Jung

Dreams and Philosophy

Carl Gustav Jung (July 26, 1875, Kesswil – June 6, 1961, Küsnacht) was a Swiss psychiatrist, influential thinker, and founder of analytical psychology.

Jung's unique and broadly influential approach to psychology has emphasized understanding the psyche through exploring the worlds of dreams, art, mythology, world religion and philosophy. Although he was a theoretical psychologist and practicing clinician for most of his life, much of his life's work was spent exploring other realms, including Eastern and Western philosophy, alchemy, astrology, sociology, as well as literature and the arts. His most notable contributions include his concept of the Jungian archetype, the collective unconscious, and his theory of synchronicity.

Jung emphasized the importance of balance and harmony. He cautioned that modern humans rely too heavily on science and logic and would benefit from integrating spirituality and appreciation of the unconscious realm.

Biography

Early Years

Carl Jung was born Karl Gustav II Jung[1] on July 26, 1875 in Kesswil, in the Swiss canton (state) of Thurgau, as the fourth but only surviving child of Paul Achilles Jung and Emilie Preiswerk. His father, Paul Jung, was a poor rural parson in the Swiss Reformed Church while his mother, Emilie, came from a wealthy, established Swiss family.

When Carl was six months old, Paul Jung acquired a position at a better parsonage in Laufen and the family moved there. Meanwhile, the tension between Paul and Emilie was growing. An eccentric and depressed woman, Emilie spent

Dreams and Philosophy

Carl Jung – Dreams and Philosophy
is available for free download at
www.biographiq.com/bookd/CJDP458

Filiquarian Publishing, LLC.

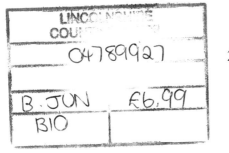
2

much of the time in her own separate bedroom, enthralled by the spirits that she said visited her at night. Emilie left Laufen for several months of hospitalization near Basel for an unknown physical ailment. Young Carl was taken by his father to live with Emilie's single sister in Basel, but later brought back to the vicarage. Emilie's continuing bouts of absence and often depressed mood influenced his attitude towards women — one of "innate unreliability," a view that he later called the "handicap I started off with."[2] After three years of living in Laufen, Paul Jung requested a transfer and was called to Kleinhüningen in 1879. The relocation brought Emilie in closer contact to her family and lifted her melancholy and despondent mood.

A very solitary and introverted child, Jung was convinced from childhood that he had two personalities—a modern Swiss citizen, and a personality more at home in the eighteenth century.[3] "Personality No. 1," as he termed it, was a typical schoolboy living in the era of the time, while No. 2 was a dignified, authoritative, and influential man from the past. Although Jung was close to both parents, he was rather disappointed in his father's academic approach to faith.

A number of childhood memories had made a life-long impression on him. As a boy he carved a tiny mannequin into the end of the wooden ruler from his pupil's pencil case and placed it inside the case. He then added a stone which he had painted into upper and lower halves and hid the case in the attic. Periodically he would come back to the mannequin, often bringing tiny sheets of paper with messages inscribed on them in his own secret language. This ceremonial act, he later reflected, brought him a feeling of inner peace and security. In later years, he discovered that similarities existed in this memory and the totems of native peoples like the collection of soul-stones near Arlesheim, or the tjurungas of Australia. This, he concluded, was an unconscious ritual that he did not question or understand at the time, but which was practiced in a strikingly similar way in faraway locations that he as a young boy had no way of consciously knowing about.[4] His findings on psychological archetypes and the collective unconscious were inspired in part by this experience.

Shortly before the end of his first year at the Humanistisches Gymnasium in Basel, at age 12, he was pushed unexpectedly by another boy, which knocked him to the ground so hard that he was for a moment unconscious. The thought then came to him that "now you won't have to go to school any more."[5] From then on, whenever he started off to school or began homework, he fainted. He remained at home for the next six months until he overheard his father speaking worriedly to a visitor of his future ability to support himself, as they suspected he had epilepsy. With little money in the family, this brought the boy to reality and he realized the need for academic excellence. He immediately went into his father's study and began poring over Latin grammar. He fainted three times, but eventually he overcame the urge and did not faint again. This event, Jung later recalled, "was when I learned what a neurosis is."[6]

Adolescence and Early Adulthood

Jung wanted to study archaeology at university, but his family was not wealthy enough to send him further afield than Basel, where they did not teach this subject, so instead Jung studied medicine at the University of Basel from 1894 to 1900. The formerly introverted student became much more lively here. In 1903, Jung married Emma Rauschenbach, from one of the richest families in Switzerland.

Towards the end of studies, his reading of Krafft-Ebing persuaded him to specialize in psychiatric medicine. He later worked in the Burghölzli, a psychiatric hospital in Zürich.

In 1906, he published Studies in Word Association and later sent a copy of this book to famed psychoanalyst Sigmund Freud, after which a close friendship between these two men followed for some 6 years (see section on Jung and Freud). In 1912 Jung published Wandlungen und Symbole der Libido (known in English as The Psychology of the Unconscious) resulting in a theoretical divergence between Jung and Freud and consequently a break in their friendship, both stating that the other was unable to admit he could possibly be wrong. After this falling-out, Jung went through a pivotal and difficult psychological transformation, which was exacerbated by news of the First World War. Henri Ellenberger called Jung's experience a "creative illness" and compared it to Freud's period of what he called neurasthenia and hysteria.

Later Life

Following World War I, Jung became a worldwide traveler, facilitated by his wife's inherited fortune as well as the funds he received through psychiatric fees, book sales, and honoraria. He visited Northern Africa shortly after, and New Mexico and Kenya in the mid-1920s. In 1938, he delivered the Terry Lectures, Psychology and Religion, at Yale University. It was at about this stage in his life that Jung visited India. His experience in India led him to become fascinated and deeply involved with Eastern philosophies and religions, helping him come up with key concepts of his ideology, including integrating spirituality into daily life and appreciation of the unconscious.

Jung's marriage with Emma produced five children and lasted until Emma's death in 1955, but she certainly experienced emotional trauma, brought about by Jung's relationships with other women. The most well-known women with whom Jung is believed to have had extramarital affairs were patient and friend Sabina Spielrein[7] and Toni Wolff.[8] Jung continued to publish books until the end of his life, including a work showing his late interest in flying saucers. He also enjoyed a friendship with an English Catholic priest, Father Victor White, who corresponded with Jung after he had published his controversial Answer to Job.[9]

Jung's work on himself and his patients convinced him that life has a spiritual purpose beyond material goals. Our main task, he believed, is to discover and fulfill our deep-innate potential, much as the acorn contains the potential to become the oak, or the caterpillar to become the butterfly. Based on his study of Christianity, Hinduism, Buddhism, Gnosticism, Taoism, and other traditions, Jung perceived that this journey of transformation is at the mystical heart of all religions. It is a journey to meet the self and at the same time to meet the Divine. Unlike Sigmund Freud, Jung thought spiritual experience was essential to our well-being. [10]

Jung died in 1961 in Zürich, after a short illness.

Jung and Freud

Jung was thirty when he sent his work Studies in Word Association to Sigmund Freud in Vienna. The first conversation between Jung and Freud lasted over 13 hours. Half a year later, the then 50 year old Freud reciprocated by sending a collection of his latest published essays to Jung in Zürich, which marked the beginning of an intense correspondence and collaboration that lasted more than six years and ended shortly before World War I in May 1910, when Jung resigned as the chairman of the International Psychoanalytical Association.

Today Jung's and Freud's theories influence different schools of psychiatry, but, more importantly, they influenced each other during intellectually formative years of their lives. In 1906 psychoanalysis as an institution was still in its early developmental stages. Jung, who had become interested in psychiatry as a student by reading Psychopathia Sexualis by Richard von

Krafft-Ebing, professor in Vienna, now worked as a doctor under the psychiatrist Eugen Bleuler in the Burghölzli and became familiar with Freud's idea of the unconscious through Freud's The Interpretation of Dreams (1900) and was a proponent of the new "psycho-analysis". At the time, Freud needed collaborators and pupils to validate and spread his ideas. The Burghölzli was a renowned psychiatric clinic in Zürich at which Jung was an up-and-coming young doctor.

In 1908, Jung became editor of the newly founded Yearbook for Psychoanalytical and Psychopathological Research. The following year, Jung traveled with Freud and Sandor Ferenczi to the U.S. to spread the news of psychoanalysis and in 1910, Jung became chairman for life of the International Psychoanalytical Association. While Jung worked on his Wandlungen und Symbole der Libido (Psychology of the Unconscious), tensions grew between Freud and Jung, due in a large part to their disagreements over the nature of libido and religion. In 1912 these tensions came to a peak because Jung felt severely slighted after Freud visited his colleague Ludwig Binswanger in Kreuzlingen without paying him a visit in nearby

Zürich, an incident Jung referred to as the Kreuzlingen gesture. Shortly thereafter, Jung again traveled to the U.S.A. and gave the Fordham lectures, which were published as The Theory of Psychoanalysis, and while they contain some remarks on Jung's dissenting view on the nature of libido, they represent largely a "psychoanalytical Jung" and not the theory Jung became famous for in the following decades.

In November 1912, Jung and Freud met in Munich for a meeting among prominent colleagues to discuss psychoanalytical journals.[11]. At a talk about a new psychoanalytic essay on Amenhotep IV, Jung expressed his views on how it related to actual conflicts in the psychoanalytic movement. While Jung spoke, Freud suddenly fainted and Jung carried him to a couch.

Jung and Freud personally met for the last time in September 1913 for the Fourth International Psychoanalytical Congress, also in Munich. Jung gave a talk on psychological types, the introverted and the extraverted type, in analytical psychology. This constituted the introduction of some of the key concepts which came to distinguish Jung's work from Freud's in the next half century.

In the following years Jung experienced considerable isolation in his professional life, exacerbated through World War I. His Seven Sermons to the Dead (1917) reprinted in his autobiography Memories, Dreams, Reflections (see bibliography) can also be read as expression of the psychological conflicts which beset Jung around the age of forty after the break with Freud.

Jung's primary disagreement with Freud stemmed from their differing concepts of the unconscious. Jung saw Freud's theory of the unconscious as incomplete and unnecessarily negative. According to Jung (though not according to Freud), Freud conceived the unconscious solely as a repository of repressed emotions and desires. Jung agreed with Freud's model of the unconscious, what Jung called the 'personal unconscious,' but he also proposed the existence of a second, far deeper form of the unconscious underlying the personal one. This was the collective unconscious, where the archetypes themselves resided, represented in mythology by a lake, or body of water, and in some cases a jug or other container.

Jung and Nazism

Though the field of psychoanalysis was dominated at the time by Jewish practitioners, and Jung had many friends and respected colleagues who were Jewish, a shadow hung over Jung's career due to allegations that he was a Nazi sympathizer. Jung was editor of the Zentralblatt für Psychotherapie, a publication that eventually endorsed Mein Kampf as required reading for all psychoanalysts. Jung claimed this was done to save psychoanalysis and preserve it during the war, believing that psychoanalysis would not otherwise survive because the Nazis considered it to be a "Jewish science." He also claimed he did it with the help and support of his Jewish friends and colleagues.[12] This after-the-fact explanation, however, has been strongly challenged on the basis of available documents.[13] The question remains unresolved.

Jung also served as president of the Nazi-dominated International General Medical Society for Psychotherapy. One of his first acts as president was to modify the constitution so that German Jewish doctors could maintain their membership as individual members even though they were excluded from all German medical societies. Also, in 1934 when he presented his paper "A Review of the Complex Theory," in his presidential address he did not discount the importance of Freud and credited him with as much influence as he could possibly give to an old mentor. Later in the war, Jung resigned. In addition, in 1943 he aided the Office of Strategic Services by analyzing Nazi leaders for the United States.[14] See also ongoing discussion in relation to 'post-Jungian' interpretation[15]

Influence

Jung has had an enduring influence on psychology as well as wider society. He has influenced psychotherapy (see Jungian psychology and analytical psychology).

* The concept of introversion vs. extraversion

* The concept of the complex

* Two typologies, Myers-Briggs Type Indicator (MBTI) and Socionics, were inspired by Jung's psychological types theory.

* Archetype concept, as an element of the archaic common substratum of the mind, or Collective Unconscious mind.

* Synchronicity idea, as an alternative to the Causality Principle, that has influence even on modern physicists.

Spirituality as a Cure for Alcoholism

Jung's influence can sometimes be found in more unexpected quarters. For example, Jung once treated an American patient (Rowland H.) suffering from chronic alcoholism. After working with the patient for some time, and achieving no significant progress, Jung told the man that his alcoholic condition was near to hopeless, save only the possibility of a spiritual experience. Jung noted that occasionally such experiences had been known to reform alcoholics where all else had failed.

Rowland took Jung's advice seriously and set about seeking a personal spiritual experience. He returned home to the United States and joined a Christian evangelical movement known as the Oxford Group. He also told other alcoholics what Jung had told him about the importance of a spiritual experience. One of the alcoholics he told was Ebby Thacher, a long-time friend and drinking buddy of Bill Wilson, later co-founder of Alcoholics Anonymous (AA). Thacher told Wilson about Jung's ideas. Wilson, who was finding it impossible to maintain sobriety, was impressed and sought out his own spiritual experience. The influence of Jung thus indirectly found its way into the formation of Alcoholics Anonymous, the original 12-step program, and from there into the whole 12-step recovery movement, although AA as a whole is not Jungian and Jung had no role in the formation of that approach or the 12 steps.

The above claims are documented in the letters of Carl Jung and Bill W., excerpts of which can be found in Pass It On, published by Alcoholics Anonymous.[16] Although the detail of this story is disputed by some historians, Jung himself made reference to its substance -- including the Oxford Group participation of the individual in question -- in a talk that was issued privately in 1954 as a transcript from shorthand taken by an attendee (Jung reportedly approved the transcript), later recorded in Volume 18 of his Collected Works, The Symbolic Life ("For instance, when a member of the Oxford Group comes to me in order to get treatment, I say, 'You are in the Oxford Group; so long as you are there, you settle your affair with the Oxford Group. I can't do it better than Jesus.' I will tell you a story of such a case. A hysterical alcoholic was cured by this Group movement..."[17])

Influences on Culture

Literature

* Jung had a 16-year long friendship with author Laurens van der Post from which a number of books and a film were created about Jung's life.[18]

* Herman Hesse, author of works such as Siddhartha and Der Steppenwolf, was treated by a student of Jung, Dr. Joseph Lang. This began for Hesse a long preoccupation with psychoanalysis, through which he came to know Carl Jung personally.[19]

* James Joyce in his Finnegans Wake, asks "Is the Co-education of Animus and Anima Wholly Desirable?" his answer perhaps being contained in his line "anama anamaba anamabapa." The book also ridicules Carl Jung's analytical psychology and Sigmund Freud's psychoanalysis, by referring to "psoakoonaloose." Jung had been unable to help Joyce's daughter Lucia, who Joyce claimed was a girl "yung and easily freudened." Lucia was diagnosed as schizophrenic and was eventually permanently institutionalized.[20]

* Joyce's A Portrait of the Artist as a Young Man can be read as an ironic parody of Jung's "four stages of eroticism." See Hiromi Yoshida, Joyce & Jung: The "Four Stages of Eroticism" in A Portrait of the Artist as a Young Man (New York: Peter Lang, 2007).

* Jung's differentiation between sensing, intuition, thinking, and feeling inspired the categorization of two of the four delineating factors in the Myers-Briggs personality test. These are the "N" (intuition) vs. "S" (sensing) and "T" (thinking) vs. "F" (feeling) groupings.

* Jung's influence on noted Canadian novelist Robertson Davies is apparent in many of Davies's fictional works. In particular, The Cornish Trilogy and his novel The Manticore base their designs on Jungian concepts.

* Jung appears as a character in the novel Possessing the Secret of Joy by Alice Walker. He appears as the therapist of Tashi, the novel's protagonist. He is usually called "Mzee," but is identified by Alice Walker in the afterword.[21]

* In the novel "Pilgrim" by Timothy Findley Carl Jung has a fictional main role where he is treating a suicide who believes he has lived many lifetimes.

Art

* The visionary Swiss painter Peter Birkhäuser was treated by a student of Jung, Marie-Louise von Franz, and corresponded with Jung regarding the translation of dream symbolism into works of art.[22]

* American Abstract Expressionist Jackson Pollock underwent Jungian analysis. Archetypal images crept into his work as he moved from representational forms to his classic "drip paintings."

Television and Film

* Dr. Niles Crane on the popular television sitcom Frasier is a devoted Jungian psychiatrist, while his brother Dr. Frasier Crane is a Freudian psychiatrist. This is mentioned a number of times in the series, and from time to time forms a point of argument between the two brothers. One memorable scene had Niles filling in for Frasier on Frasier's call-in radio program, in which Niles introduces himself as the temporary substitute saying, "...and while my brother is a Freudian, I

am a Jungian, so there'll be no blaming Mother today."

* Jung and his ideas are mentioned often, and sometimes play an integral role, in the television series Northern Exposure. Jung even makes an appearance in one of the character's dreams.

Music

* Jung appears on the cover of The Beatles' Sgt. Pepper's Lonely Hearts Club Band.

* Peter Gabriel's song "Rhythm Of The Heat" (Security, 1982), tells about psychologist Carl Jung's visit to Africa, during which he joined a group of tribal drummers and dancers and became overwhelmed by the fear of losing control of himself. At the time, Jung was exploring the concept of the Collective Unconscious, and was afraid he would come under control of the music, as the drummers and dancers let the music control them in fulfillment of their ritual objectives. Gabriel learned about Jung's journey to Africa from Jung's essay Symbols And The Interpretation Of Dreams (ISBN 0-691-09968-5). In his song,

Gabriel tries to capture the powerful feelings the African tribal music evoked in Jung by means of intense use of tribal drumbeats. The original song title was Jung in Africa.[23]

* The British pop band The Police's final album, Synchronicity, contains numerous allusions to Jung; the album cover prominently depicts bassist Sting reading a copy of Jung's work.

* The band Saigon Kick makes a reference to Jung in I Love You, saying "I may not have the mind of Jung".

* Alternative/metal band Tool uses many allusions to Jungian psychology throughout many of their works.

Notes and References

1. As a university student Jung changed the modernized spelling of his name to the original family form. Bair, Deirdre (2003). Jung: A Biography. New York: Back Bay Books, pp. 7–8,53. ISBN 0-316-15938-7.

2. Jung, C.G.; Aniela Jaffé (1965). Memories, Dreams, Reflections. New York: Random House, p. 8.

3. Memories, Dreams, Reflections, pp. 33–34.

4. Memories, Dreams, Reflections, pp. 22–23.

5. Memories, Dreams, Reflections, p. 30.

6. Memories, Dreams, Reflections, p. 32.

7. Hayman, Ronald (1999). A Life of Jung. New York: W.W. Norton & Co., pp. 84-5, 92, 98-9, 102-7, 121, 123, 111, 134-7, 138-9, 145, 147, 152, 176, 177, 184, 185, 186, 189, 194, 213-4. ISBN 0393019675.

8. A Life of Jung, pp. 184-8, 189, 244, 261, 262.

9. In Psychology and Religion, v.11, Collected Works of C.G. Jung, Princeton. It was first published as "Antwort auf Hiob," Zürich, 1952 and translated into English in 1954, in London.

10. Crowley, Vivianne (2000). Jung: A Journey of Transformation:Exploring His Life and Experiencing His Ideas. Wheaton Illinois: Quest Books. ISBN 978-0835607827.

11. Jonest, Ernest, ed. Lionel Trilling and Steven Marcus. The Life and Work of Sigmund Freud New York: Anchor Books, 1963.

12. Mark Medweth, « Jung and the Nazis », in Psybernetika, Winter 1996.

13. Richard Noll (1997), 'The Aryan Christ,' Random House.

14. Article Jung, Carl Gustav in Columbia Encyclopedia, 6th ed.

15. ArticleThe Recent Attacks on Jung: Answer to the Post-Jungians

16. Alcoholics Anonymous World Services, Inc. (1984) Pass It On: The Story of Bill Wilson and how the A.A. message reached the world. New York: Alcoholics Anonymous World Services, Inc. ISBN 0-916856-12-7, pp. 381-386

17. Jung, C. G.; Adler, G. and Hull, R. F. C., eds. (1977) Collected Works of C. G. Jung, Volume 18: The Symbolic Life: Miscellaneous Writings, Princeton, NJ: Princeton University Press, ISBN 978-0-691-09892-0, p. 272, as noted 2007-08-26 at http://www.stellarfire.org/additional.html

18. "Laurens van der Post" (HTML). Retrieved on 2007-12-02.

19. "Hermann Hesse" (HTML). Retrieved on 2007-12-02.

20. Bair, Deirdre. Jung: A Biography.

21. "Possessing the Secret of Joy" (HTML). Retrieved on 2007-12-02.

22. Birkhäuser, Peter; Marie-Louise von Franz, Eva Wertanschlag and Kaspar Birkhäuser (1980-1991). Light from the Darkness: The Paintings of Peter Birkhäuser. Boston, MA: Birkhäuser Verlag. ISBN 3764311908.

23. "Rhythm Of The Heat by Peter Gabriel", Song Facts (HTML). Retrieved on 2006-12-16.

Further Reading

There is much literature on Jungian thought. For a good, short and easily accessible introduction to Jung's thought:

* Chapter 1 of Man and His Symbols, conceived and edited by Jung.

Other good introductory texts include:

* The Portable Jung, edited by Joseph Campbell (Viking Portable), ISBN 0-14-015070-6

* Edward F Edinger, Ego and Archetype, (Shambala), ISBN 0-87773-576-X

* Another recommended tool for navigating Jung's works is Robert Hopcke's book, A Guided Tour of the Collected Works of C.G. Jung, ISBN 1-57062-405-4. He offers short, lucid summaries of all of Jung's major ideas and suggests readings from Jung's and others' work that best present that idea.

* Edward C. Whitmont, The Symbolic Quest: Basic Concepts of Analytical Psychology, Princeton University Press, Princeton, New Jersey, 1969, 1979, ISBN 0-691-02454-5

* Anthony Stevens, Jung. A Very Short Introduction, Oxford University Press, Oxford, 1994, ISBN 0-19-285458-5

* O'Connor, Peter A. (1985). Understanding Jung, understanding yourself. New York, NY: Paulist Press. ISBN 0 809127997.

Good texts in various areas of Jungian thought:

* Robert Aziz, C.G. Jung's Psychology of Religion and Synchronicity (1990), currently in its 10th printing, is a refereed publication of The

State University of New York Press. ISBN 0-7914-0166-9.

* Robert Aziz, Synchronicity and the Transformation of the Ethical in Jungian Psychology in Carl B. Becker, ed. Asian and Jungian Views of Ethics. Westport, CT: Greenwood, 1999. ISBN 0-313-30452-1.

* Robert Aziz, The Syndetic Paradigm:The Untrodden Path Beyond Freud and Jung (2007), a refereed publication of The State University of New York Press. ISBN 13:978-0-7914-6982-8.

* Edward F. Edinger, The Mystery of The Coniunctio, ISBN 0-919123-67-8. A good explanation of Jung's foray into the symbolism of alchemy as it relates to individuation and individual religious experience. Many of the alchemical symbols recur in contemporary dreams (with creative additions from the unconscious e.g. space travel, internet, computers)

* James A Hall M.D., Jungian Dream Interpretation, ISBN 0-919123-12-0. A brief, well

structured overview of the use of dreams in
therapy.

* James Hillman, "Healing Fiction", ISBN 0-
88214-363-8. Covers Jung, Adler, and Freud and
their various contributions to understanding the
soul.

* Andrew Samuels, Critical Dictionary of Jungian
Analysis, ISBN 0-415-05910-0

* June Singer, Boundaries of the Soul, ISBN 0-
385-47529-2. On psychotherapy

* Marion Woodman, The Pregnant Virgin: A
Process of Psychological Transformation ISBN 0-
919123-20-1. The recovery of feminine values in
women (and men). There are many examples of
clients' dreams, by an experienced analyst.

* Frederic Fappani," Education and Archetypal
Psychology ", Ed.Cursus, Paris.

 And a more academic text:

* Andrew Samuels, The Political Psyche (Routledge), ISBN 0-415-08102-5. Difficult, but useful.

For the Jung-Freud relationship:

* Kerr, John. A Most Dangerous Method : The Story of Jung, Freud, and Sabina Spielrein. Knopf 1993. ISBN 0-679-40412-0.

For critical scholarship on Jung from the perspective of historians of psychiatry:

* Richard Noll, The Jung Cult: Origins of a Charismatic Movement (Princeton University Press, 1994); and

* Richard Noll, The Aryan Christ: The Secret Life of Carl Jung (Random House, 1997)[1]

* Sonu Shamdasani, Cult Fictions, ISBN 0-415-18614-5. Critique of the above works by Noll.

* Sonu Shamdasani, Jung and the Making of Modern Psychology : The Dream of a Science, ISBN 0-521-53909-9. A comprehensive study of

the origins of Jung's psychology which places it in a historical and philosophical context. The author calls this a "Cubist history".

* Sonu Shamdasani, Jung Stripped Bare, ISBN 1-85575-317-0. Critique of Jung biographies.

* Bair, Deirdre. Jung: A Biography. Boston: Little, Brown and Co, 2003.

Jung Bibliography

Works arranged by original publication date if known:

* Jung, C. G. (1902–1905). Psychiatric Studies. The Collected Works of C. G. Jung Vol.1. 1953, ed. Michael Fordham, London: Routledge & Kegan Paul, and Princeton, N.J.: Bollingen. This was the first of 18 volumes plus separate bibliography and index. Not including revisions the set was completed in 1967.

* Jung, C. G. (1904–1907) Studies in Word Association. London: Routledge & K. Paul.

(contained in Experimental Researches, Collected Works Vol. 2)

* Jung, C. G. (1907). The Psychology of Dementia Praecox. (2nd ed. 1936) New York: Nervous and Mental Disease Publ. Co. (contained in The Psychogenesis of Mental Disease, Collected Works Vol.3. This is the disease now known as schizophrenia)

* Jung, C. G. (1907–1958). The Psychogenesis of Mental Disease. 1991 ed. London: Routledge. (Collected Works Vol. 3)

* Jung, C. G., & Hinkle, B. M. (1912). Psychology of the Unconscious : a study of the transformations and symbolisms of the libido, a contribution to the history of the evolution of thought. London: Kegan Paul Trench Trubner. (revised in 1952 as Symbols of Transformation, Collected Works Vol.5 ISBN 0-691-01815-4)

* Jung, C. G., & Long, C. E. (1917). Collected Papers on Analytical Psychology (2nd ed.). London: Balliere Tindall & Cox. (contained in

Freud and Psychoanalysis, Collected Works Vol. 4)

* Jung, C. G. (1917, 1928). Two Essays on Analytical Psychology (1966 revised 2nd ed. Collected Works Vol. 7). London: Routledge.

* Jung, C. G., & Baynes, H. G. (1921). Psychological Types, or, The Psychology of Individuation. London: Kegan Paul Trench Trubner. (Collected Works Vol.6 ISBN 0-691-01813-8)

* Jung, C. G., Baynes, H. G., & Baynes, C. F. (1928). Contributions to Analytical Psychology. London: Routledge & Kegan Paul.

* Jung, C. G., & Shamdasani, S. (1932). The Psychology of Kundalini Yoga: notes of a seminar by C.G. Jung. 1996 ed. Princeton, N.J.: Princeton University Press.

* Jung, C. G. (1933). Modern Man in Search of a Soul. London: Kegan Paul Trench Trubner, (1955 ed. Harvest Books ISBN 0-15-661206-2)

* Jung, C. G., (1934–1954). The Archetypes and The Collective Unconscious. (1981 2nd ed. Collected Works Vol.9 Part 1), Princeton, N.J.: Bollingen. ISBN 0-691-01833-2

* Jung, C. G. (1938). Psychology and Religion The Terry Lectures. New Haven: Yale University Press. (contained in Psychology and Religion: West and East Collected Works Vol. 11 ISBN 0-691-09772-0).

* Jung, C. G., & Dell, S. M. (1940). The Integration of the Personality. London: Routledge and Kegan Paul.

* Jung, C. G. (1944). Psychology and Alchemy (2nd ed. 1968 Collected Works Vol. 12 ISBN 0-691-01831-6). London: Routledge.

* Jung, C. G. (1947). Essays on Contemporary Events. London: Kegan Paul.

* Jung, C. G. (1947, revised 1954). On the Nature of the Psyche. 1988 ed. London: Ark Paperbacks. (contained in Collected Works Vol. 8)

* Jung, C.G. (1949). Foreword, pp. xxi-xxxix (19 pages), to Wilhelm/Baynes translation of The I Ching or Book of Changes. Bollingen Edition XIX, Princeton University Press.(contained in Collected Works Vol. 11)

* Jung, C. G. (1951). Aion: Researches into the Phenomenology of the Self (Collected Works Vol. 9 Part 2). Princeton, N.J.: Bollingen. ISBN 0-691-01826-X

* Jung, C. G. (1952). Synchronicity: An Acausal Connecting Principle. 1973 2nd ed. Princeton, N.J.: Princeton University Press, ISBN 0-691-01794-8 (contained in Collected Works Vol. 8)

* Jung, C. G. (1956). Mysterium Coniunctionis: An Inquiry into the Separation and Synthesis of Psychic Opposites in Alchemy. London: Routledge. (2nd ed. 1970 Collected Works Vol. 14 ISBN 0-691-01816-2) This was Jung's last book length work, completed when he was eighty.

* Jung, C. G. (1957). The Undiscovered Self (Present and Future). 1959 ed. New York: American Library. 1990 ed. Bollingen ISBN 0-

691-01894-4 (50 p. essay, also contained in collected Works Vol. 10)

* Jung, C. G., & De Laszlo, V. S. (1958). Psyche and Symbol: A Selection from the Writings of C.G. Jung. Garden City, N.Y.: Doubleday.

* Jung, C. G., & De Laszlo, V. S. (1959). Basic Writings. New York: Modern Library.

* Jung, C. G., & Jaffe A. (1962). Memories, Dreams, Reflections. London: Collins. This is Jung's autobiography, recorded and edited by Aniela Jaffe, ISBN 0-679-72395-1

* Jung, C. G., Evans, R. I., & Jones, E. (1964). Conversations with Carl Jung and Reactions from Ernest Jones. New York: Van Nostrand.

* Jung, C. G., & Franz, M.-L. v. (1964). Man and His Symbols. Garden City, N.Y.: Doubleday, ISBN 0-440-35183-9

* Jung, C. G. (1966). The Practice of Psychotherapy: Essays on the Psychology of the Transference and other Subjects (Collected Works

Vol. 16). Princeton, N.J.: Princeton University Press.

* Jung, C. G. (1967). The Development of Personality. 1991 ed. London: Routledge. Collected Works Vol. 17 ISBN 0-691-01838-3

* Jung, C. G. (1970). Four Archetypes; Mother, Rebirth, Spirit, Trickster. Princeton, N.J.: Princeton University Press. (contained in Collected Works Vol. 9 part 1)

* Jung, C. G. (1974). Dreams. Princeton, N.J.: Princeton University Press (compilation from Collected Works Vols. 4, 8, 12, 16), ISBN 0-691-01792-1

* Jung, C. G., & Campbell, J. (1976). The Portable Jung. a compilation, New York: Penguin Books. ISBN 0-14-015070-6

* Jung, C. G., Rothgeb, C. L., Clemens, S. M., & National Clearinghouse for Mental Health Information (U.S.). (1978). Abstracts of the Collected Works of C.G. Jung. Washington, D.C.: U.S. Govt. Printing Office.

* Jung, C. G., & Antony Storr ed., (1983) The Essential Jung. a compilation, Princeton, N.J.: Princeton University Press, ISBN 0-691-02455-3

* Jung, C. G. (1986). Psychology and the East. London: Ark. (contained in Collected Works Vol. 11)

* Jung, C. G. (1987). Dictionary of Analytical Psychology. London: Ark Paperbacks.

* Jung, C. G. (1988). Psychology and Western Religion. London: Ark Paperbacks. (contained in Collected Works Vol. 11)

* Jung, C. G., Wagner, S., Wagner, G., & Van der Post, L. (1990). The World Within C.G. Jung in his own words [videorecording]. New York, NY: Kino International : Dist. by Insight Media.

* Jung, C. G., & Hull, R. F. C. (1991). Psychological Types (a revised ed.). London: Routlege.

* Jung, C. G., & Chodorow, J. (1997). Jung on Active Imagination. Princeton, N.J.: Princeton University Press.

* Jung, C. G., & Jarrett, J. L. (1998). Jung's Seminar on Nietzsche's Zarathustra (Abridged ed.). Princeton, N.J.: Princeton University Press.

* Jung, C. G., & Pauli, Wolfgang, C. A. Meier (Editor). (2001). Atom and Archetype : The Pauli/Jung Letters, 1932-1958, Princeton, N.J.: Princeton University Press. ISBN 0-691-01207-5

* Jung, C. G., & Sabini, M. (2002). The Earth Has a Soul: the nature writings of C.G. Jung. Berkeley, Calif.: North Atlantic Books.

* Anthony Stevens. "Jung, A Very Short Introduction" (1994)

An early writing by Jung, dating from around 1917, was his poetic work, The Seven Sermons To The Dead (Full Text). Written in the persona of the 2nd century religious teacher Basilides of Alexandria, it explores ancient religious and spiritual themes, including those of gnosticism.

This work is included in some editions of Memories, Dreams, Reflections.

Carl Jung

GNU Free Documentation License

Version 1.2, November 2002

0. PREAMBLE

The purpose of this License is to make a manual, textbook, or other functional and useful document "free" in the sense of freedom: to assure everyone the effective freedom to copy and redistribute it, with or without modifying it, either commercially or noncommercially. Secondarily, this License preserves for the author and publisher a way to get credit for their work, while not being considered responsible for modifications made by others.

This License is a kind of "copyleft", which means that derivative works of the document must themselves be free in the same sense. It complements the GNU General Public License, which is a copyleft license designed for free software.

We have designed this License in order to use it for manuals for free software, because free software needs free documentation: a free program should come with manuals providing the same freedoms that the software does. But this License is not limited to software manuals; it can be used for any textual work, regardless of subject matter or whether it is published as a printed book. We recommend this License principally for works whose purpose is instruction or reference.

Dreams and Philosophy

1. APPLICABILITY AND DEFINITIONS

This License applies to any manual or other work, in any medium, that contains a notice placed by the copyright holder saying it can be distributed under the terms of this License. Such a notice grants a world-wide, royalty-free license, unlimited in duration, to use that work under the conditions stated herein. The "Document", below, refers to any such manual or work. Any member of the public is a licensee, and is addressed as "you". You accept the license if you copy, modify or distribute the work in a way requiring permission under copyright law.

A "Modified Version" of the Document means any work containing the Document or a portion of it, either copied verbatim, or with modifications and/or translated into another language.

A "Secondary Section" is a named appendix or a front-matter section of the Document that deals exclusively with the relationship of the publishers or authors of the Document to the Document's overall subject (or to related matters) and contains nothing that could fall directly within that overall subject. (Thus, if the Document is in part a textbook of mathematics, a Secondary Section may not explain any mathematics.) The relationship could be a matter of historical connection with the subject or with related matters, or of legal, commercial, philosophical, ethical or political position regarding them.

The "Invariant Sections" are certain Secondary Sections whose titles are designated, as being those of Invariant Sections, in the notice that says that the Document is released under this License. If a section does not fit the above definition of Secondary then it is not allowed to be designated as Invariant. The Document may contain zero Invariant Sections. If the Document does not identify any Invariant Sections then there are none.

The "Cover Texts" are certain short passages of text that are listed, as Front-Cover Texts or Back-Cover Texts, in the notice that says that the Document is released under this License. A Front-Cover Text may be at most 5 words, and a Back-Cover Text may be at most 25 words.

Carl Jung

A "Transparent" copy of the Document means a machine-readable copy, represented in a format whose specification is available to the general public, that is suitable for revising the document straightforwardly with generic text editors or (for images composed of pixels) generic paint programs or (for drawings) some widely available drawing editor, and that is suitable for input to text formatters or for automatic translation to a variety of formats suitable for input to text formatters. A copy made in an otherwise Transparent file format whose markup, or absence of markup, has been arranged to thwart or discourage subsequent modification by readers is not Transparent. An image format is not Transparent if used for any substantial amount of text. A copy that is not "Transparent" is called "Opaque".

Examples of suitable formats for Transparent copies include plain ASCII without markup, Texinfo input format, LaTeX input format, SGML or XML using a publicly available DTD, and standard-conforming simple HTML, PostScript or PDF designed for human modification. Examples of transparent image formats include PNG, XCF and JPG. Opaque formats include proprietary formats that can be read and edited only by proprietary word processors, SGML or XML for which the DTD and/or processing tools are not generally available, and the machine-generated HTML, PostScript or PDF produced by some word processors for output purposes only.

The "Title Page" means, for a printed book, the title page itself, plus such following pages as are needed to hold, legibly, the material this License requires to appear in the title page. For works in formats which do not have any title page as such, "Title Page" means the text near the most prominent appearance of the work's title, preceding the beginning of the body of the text.

A section "Entitled XYZ" means a named subunit of the Document whose title either is precisely XYZ or contains XYZ in parentheses following text that translates XYZ in another language. (Here XYZ stands for a specific section name mentioned below, such as "Acknowledgements", "Dedications", "Endorsements", or "History".) To "Preserve the Title" of such a section when you modify the Document means that it remains a section "Entitled XYZ" according to this definition.

Dreams and Philosophy

The Document may include Warranty Disclaimers next to the notice which states that this License applies to the Document. These Warranty Disclaimers are considered to be included by reference in this License, but only as regards disclaiming warranties: any other implication that these Warranty Disclaimers may have is void and has no effect on the meaning of this License.

2. VERBATIM COPYING

You may copy and distribute the Document in any medium, either commercially or noncommercially, provided that this License, the copyright notices, and the license notice saying this License applies to the Document are reproduced in all copies, and that you add no other conditions whatsoever to those of this License. You may not use technical measures to obstruct or control the reading or further copying of the copies you make or distribute. However, you may accept compensation in exchange for copies. If you distribute a large enough number of copies you must also follow the conditions in section 3.

You may also lend copies, under the same conditions stated above, and you may publicly display copies.

3. COPYING IN QUANTITY

If you publish printed copies (or copies in media that commonly have printed covers) of the Document, numbering more than 100, and the Document's license notice requires Cover Texts, you must enclose the copies in covers that carry, clearly and legibly, all these Cover Texts: Front-Cover Texts on the front cover, and Back-Cover Texts on the back cover. Both covers must also clearly and legibly identify you as the publisher of these copies. The front cover must present the full title with all words of the title equally prominent and visible. You may add other material on the covers in addition. Copying with changes limited to the covers, as long as they preserve the title of the Document and satisfy these conditions, can be treated as verbatim copying in other respects.

If the required texts for either cover are too voluminous to fit legibly, you should put the first ones listed (as many as fit reasonably) on the actual cover, and continue the rest onto adjacent pages.

Carl Jung

If you publish or distribute Opaque copies of the Document numbering more than 100, you must either include a machine-readable Transparent copy along with each Opaque copy, or state in or with each Opaque copy a computer-network location from which the general network-using public has access to download using public-standard network protocols a complete Transparent copy of the Document, free of added material. If you use the latter option, you must take reasonably prudent steps, when you begin distribution of Opaque copies in quantity, to ensure that this Transparent copy will remain thus accessible at the stated location until at least one year after the last time you distribute an Opaque copy (directly or through your agents or retailers) of that edition to the public.

It is requested, but not required, that you contact the authors of the Document well before redistributing any large number of copies, to give them a chance to provide you with an updated version of the Document.

4. MODIFICATIONS

You may copy and distribute a Modified Version of the Document under the conditions of sections 2 and 3 above, provided that you release the Modified Version under precisely this License, with the Modified Version filling the role of the Document, thus licensing distribution and modification of the Modified Version to whoever possesses a copy of it. In addition, you must do these things in the Modified Version:

* A. Use in the Title Page (and on the covers, if any) a title distinct from that of the Document, and from those of previous versions (which should, if there were any, be listed in the History section of the Document). You may use the same title as a previous version if the original publisher of that version gives permission.
* B. List on the Title Page, as authors, one or more persons or entities responsible for authorship of the modifications in the Modified Version, together with at least five of the principal authors of the Document (all of its principal authors, if it has fewer than five), unless they release you from this requirement.
* C. State on the Title page the name of the publisher of the Modified Version, as the publisher.
* D. Preserve all the copyright notices of the Document.

47

Dreams and Philosophy

* E. Add an appropriate copyright notice for your modifications adjacent to the other copyright notices.
* F. Include, immediately after the copyright notices, a license notice giving the public permission to use the Modified Version under the terms of this License, in the form shown in the Addendum below.
* G. Preserve in that license notice the full lists of Invariant Sections and required Cover Texts given in the Document's license notice.
* H. Include an unaltered copy of this License.
* I. Preserve the section Entitled "History", Preserve its Title, and add to it an item stating at least the title, year, new authors, and publisher of the Modified Version as given on the Title Page. If there is no section Entitled "History" in the Document, create one stating the title, year, authors, and publisher of the Document as given on its Title Page, then add an item describing the Modified Version as stated in the previous sentence.
* J. Preserve the network location, if any, given in the Document for public access to a Transparent copy of the Document, and likewise the network locations given in the Document for previous versions it was based on. These may be placed in the "History" section. You may omit a network location for a work that was published at least four years before the Document itself, or if the original publisher of the version it refers to gives permission.
* K. For any section Entitled "Acknowledgements" or "Dedications", Preserve the Title of the section, and preserve in the section all the substance and tone of each of the contributor acknowledgements and/or dedications given therein.
* L. Preserve all the Invariant Sections of the Document, unaltered in their text and in their titles. Section numbers or the equivalent are not considered part of the section titles.
* M. Delete any section Entitled "Endorsements". Such a section may not be included in the Modified Version.
* N. Do not retitle any existing section to be Entitled "Endorsements" or to conflict in title with any Invariant Section.
* O. Preserve any Warranty Disclaimers.

If the Modified Version includes new front-matter sections or appendices that qualify as Secondary Sections and contain no material copied from the Document, you may at your option designate some or all of these sections as invariant. To do this, add their titles to the list of Invariant Sections in the

Modified Version's license notice. These titles must be distinct from any other section titles.

You may add a section Entitled "Endorsements", provided it contains nothing but endorsements of your Modified Version by various parties--for example, statements of peer review or that the text has been approved by an organization as the authoritative definition of a standard.

You may add a passage of up to five words as a Front-Cover Text, and a passage of up to 25 words as a Back-Cover Text, to the end of the list of Cover Texts in the Modified Version. Only one passage of Front-Cover Text and one of Back-Cover Text may be added by (or through arrangements made by) any one entity. If the Document already includes a cover text for the same cover, previously added by you or by arrangement made by the same entity you are acting on behalf of, you may not add another; but you may replace the old one, on explicit permission from the previous publisher that added the old one.

The author(s) and publisher(s) of the Document do not by this License give permission to use their names for publicity for or to assert or imply endorsement of any Modified Version.

5. COMBINING DOCUMENTS

You may combine the Document with other documents released under this License, under the terms defined in section 4 above for modified versions, provided that you include in the combination all of the Invariant Sections of all of the original documents, unmodified, and list them all as Invariant Sections of your combined work in its license notice, and that you preserve all their Warranty Disclaimers.

The combined work need only contain one copy of this License, and multiple identical Invariant Sections may be replaced with a single copy. If there are multiple Invariant Sections with the same name but different contents, make the title of each such section unique by adding at the end of it, in parentheses, the name of the original author or publisher of that section if known, or else a unique number. Make the same adjustment to the section titles in the list of Invariant Sections in the license notice of the combined work.

Dreams and Philosophy

In the combination, you must combine any sections Entitled "History" in the various original documents, forming one section Entitled "History"; likewise combine any sections Entitled "Acknowledgements", and any sections Entitled "Dedications". You must delete all sections Entitled "Endorsements."

6. COLLECTIONS OF DOCUMENTS

You may make a collection consisting of the Document and other documents released under this License, and replace the individual copies of this License in the various documents with a single copy that is included in the collection, provided that you follow the rules of this License for verbatim copying of each of the documents in all other respects.

You may extract a single document from such a collection, and distribute it individually under this License, provided you insert a copy of this License into the extracted document, and follow this License in all other respects regarding verbatim copying of that document.

7. AGGREGATION WITH INDEPENDENT WORKS

A compilation of the Document or its derivatives with other separate and independent documents or works, in or on a volume of a storage or distribution medium, is called an "aggregate" if the copyright resulting from the compilation is not used to limit the legal rights of the compilation's users beyond what the individual works permit. When the Document is included in an aggregate, this License does not apply to the other works in the aggregate which are not themselves derivative works of the Document.

If the Cover Text requirement of section 3 is applicable to these copies of the Document, then if the Document is less than one half of the entire aggregate, the Document's Cover Texts may be placed on covers that bracket the Document within the aggregate, or the electronic equivalent of covers if the Document is in electronic form. Otherwise they must appear on printed covers that bracket the whole aggregate.

Carl Jung

8. TRANSLATION

Translation is considered a kind of modification, so you may distribute translations of the Document under the terms of section 4. Replacing Invariant Sections with translations requires special permission from their copyright holders, but you may include translations of some or all Invariant Sections in addition to the original versions of these Invariant Sections. You may include a translation of this License, and all the license notices in the Document, and any Warranty Disclaimers, provided that you also include the original English version of this License and the original versions of those notices and disclaimers. In case of a disagreement between the translation and the original version of this License or a notice or disclaimer, the original version will prevail.

If a section in the Document is Entitled "Acknowledgements", "Dedications", or "History", the requirement (section 4) to Preserve its Title (section 1) will typically require changing the actual title.

9. TERMINATION

You may not copy, modify, sublicense, or distribute the Document except as expressly provided for under this License. Any other attempt to copy, modify, sublicense or distribute the Document is void, and will automatically terminate your rights under this License. However, parties who have received copies, or rights, from you under this License will not have their licenses terminated so long as such parties remain in full compliance.

10. FUTURE REVISIONS OF THIS LICENSE

The Free Software Foundation may publish new, revised versions of the GNU Free Documentation License from time to time. Such new versions will be similar in spirit to the present version, but may differ in detail to address new problems or concerns. See http://www.gnu.org/copyleft/.

Each version of the License is given a distinguishing version number. If the Document specifies that a particular numbered version of this License "or any later version" applies to it, you have the option of following the terms and conditions either of that specified version or of any later version that has been published (not as a draft) by the Free Software Foundation. If the Document does not specify a version number of this License, you may choose any version ever published (not as a draft) by the Free Software Foundation.

How to use this License for your documents

To use this License in a document you have written, include a copy of the License in the document and put the following copyright and license notices just after the title page:

Copyright (c) YEAR YOUR NAME.
Permission is granted to copy, distribute and/or modify this document under the terms of the GNU Free Documentation License, Version 1.2 or any later version published by the Free Software Foundation; with no Invariant Sections, no Front-Cover Texts, and no Back-Cover Texts. A copy of the license is included in the section entitled "GNU
Free Documentation License".

If you have Invariant Sections, Front-Cover Texts and Back-Cover Texts, replace the "with...Texts." line with this:

with the Invariant Sections being LIST THEIR TITLES, with the Front-Cover Texts being LIST, and with the Back-Cover Texts being LIST.

If you have Invariant Sections without Cover Texts, or some other combination of the three, merge those two alternatives to suit the situation.

If your document contains nontrivial examples of program code, we recommend releasing these examples in parallel under your choice of free software license, such as the GNU General Public License, to permit their use in free software.

Lightning Source UK Ltd.
Milton Keynes UK
UKOW031458010312

188186UK00012B/150/P